AUTHENTIC TRANSCRIPTIONS
WITH NOTES AND TABLATURE

MW01487156

Contents

Music transcriptions by Steve Gorenberg and Jeff Jacobson

Cover photography by David Goldman

ISBN 0-634-01225-8

7777 W. BLUEMOUND RD. P.O. BOX 13819 MILWAUKEE, WI 53213

Visit Hal Leonard Online at
www.halleonard.com

Photography by Justin Steve

Dumpweed

Words and Music by Tom DeLonge and Mark Hoppus

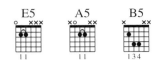

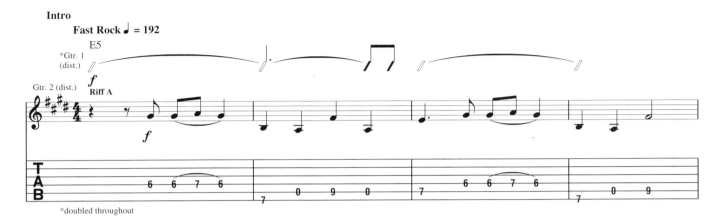

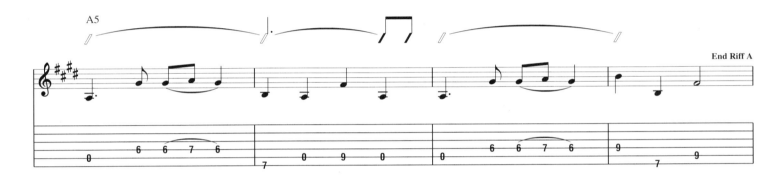

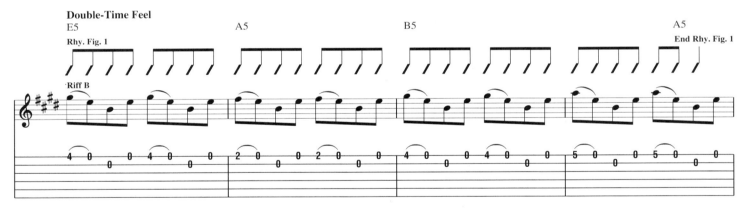

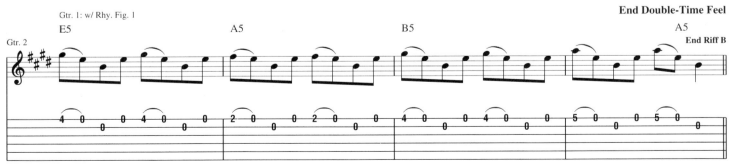

Verse

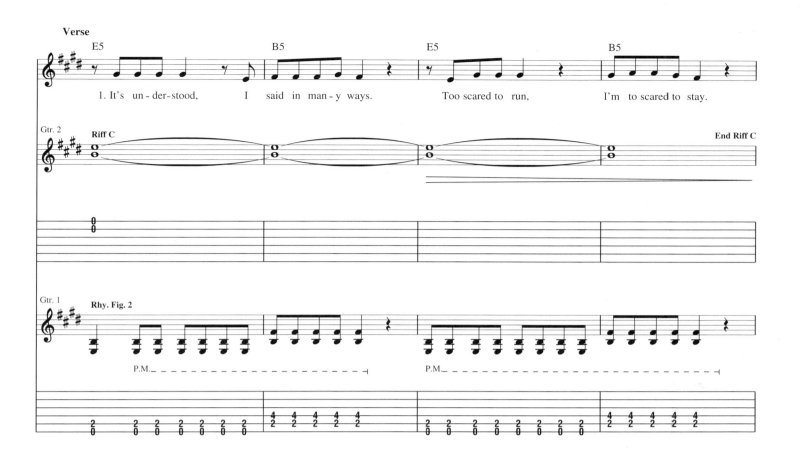

1. It's un-der-stood, I said in man-y ways. Too scared to run, I'm to scared to stay.

I said I'd leave, (but) I could nev-er leave her. (And) if I did, you know I'd nev-er cheat her.

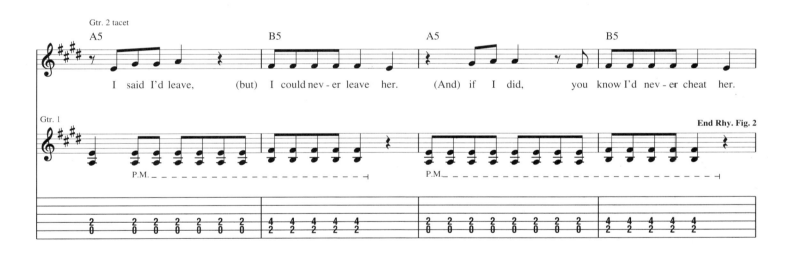

But this I ask; it's what I want to know. How would you feel if I should choose to go?

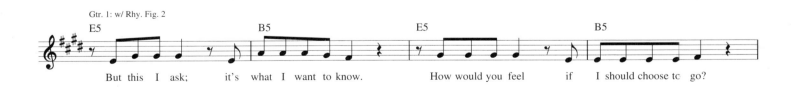

An-oth-er guy, you think it'd be un-like-ly. An-oth-er guy, you think he'd want to fight me.

Interlude

Gtr. 2: w/ Riff A, simile

Gtr. 1

E5   A5   B5

Chorus
Double-Time Feel

E5   B5   A5   B5

She's a dove, she's a fuck-in' night - mare. Un-pre-dict-a-ble, it was my mis-take to stay here.

Rhy. Fig. 3

To Coda ⊕

E5   B5   A5   B5

On the go and it's way too late to play. _ I need a girl that I can

End Rhy. Fig. 3

Interlude

Gtr. 1: w/ Rhy. Fig. 1, 2 times
Gtr. 2: w/ Riff B

E5   A5   B5   A5   E5   A5

train.

Verse

Gtr. 1: w/ Rhy. Fig. 2
End Double-Time Feel   Gtr. 2: w/ Riff C

B5   A5   E5   B5

2. I heard it once, I'm sure I heard it twice.

E5   B5   A5

My dad used to give me all of his ad-vice. He would say, "You got to

turn your back and run now.   Come on, son,   you have-n't got a chance now."

Coda

girl   that   I   can   train.   She's   a   dove,   she's   a   fuck-in'   night-mare.

Un-pre-dict-a-ble,   it was   my   mis-take   to   stay   here.   On   the   go   and   it's

End Double-Time Feel

way   too   late   to   play. ___   I   need   a   girl   that   I   can

Outro

Half-Time Feel

train.

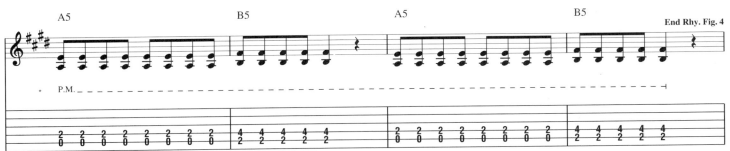

(I)   need   a   girl   that   I   can   train.   (I)   need   a   girl   that   I   can

train.   Turn your back and run now. _____   You have-n't got a chance now. _____

Gtr. 2   **Riff D**   **End Riff D**

P.M.

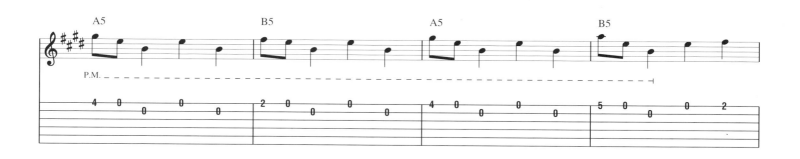

P.M.

Gtr. 2: w/ Riff D

(I) need a girl that I can train.   (I) need a girl that I can

train.   Turn your back and run now. _____   You have-n't got a chance now. _____

Gtr. 2

P.M.

Don't Leave Me

Words and Music by Tom DeLonge and Mark Hoppus

Intro
Moderate Rock ♩ = 148
Double-Time Feel

Gtr. 1: w/ Rhy. Fill 1, 2nd time

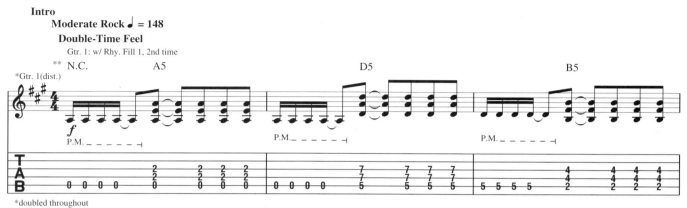

*doubled throughout
**Chord symbols reflect overall tonality.

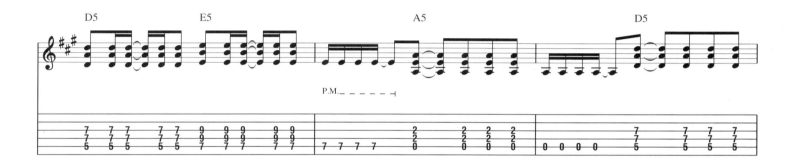

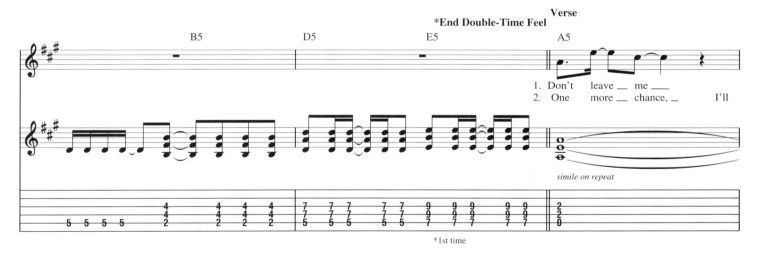

Verse
End Double-Time Feel

1. Don't leave __ me __
2. One more __ chance, __ I'll

simile on repeat

*1st time

Rhy. Fill 1
Gtr. 1

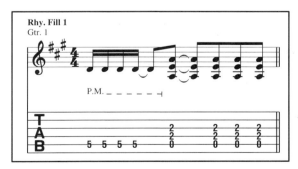

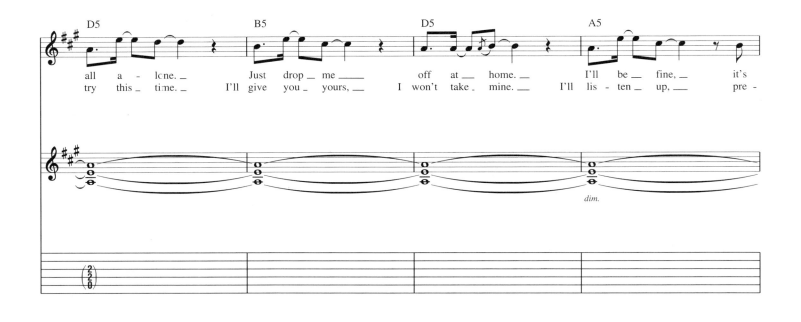

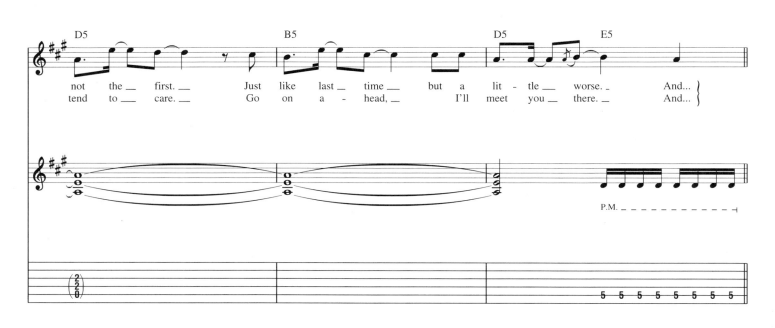

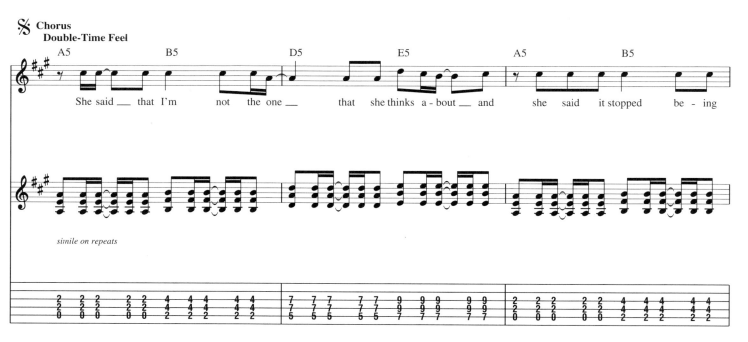

10

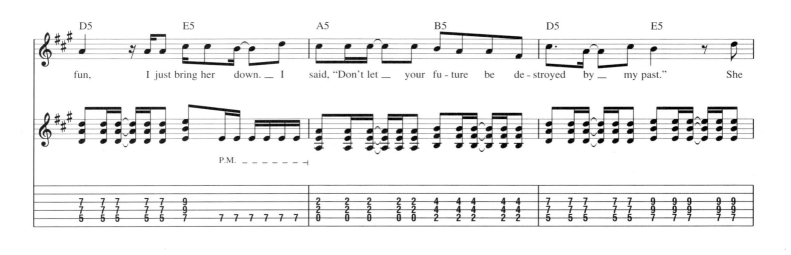

fun, I just bring her down. ___ I said, "Don't let ___ your fu-ture be de-stroyed by ___ my past." She

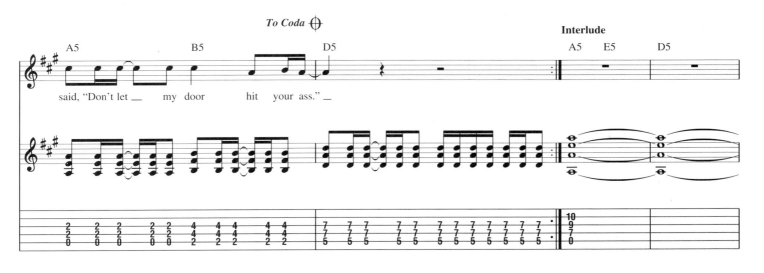

said, "Don't let ___ my door hit your ass." ___

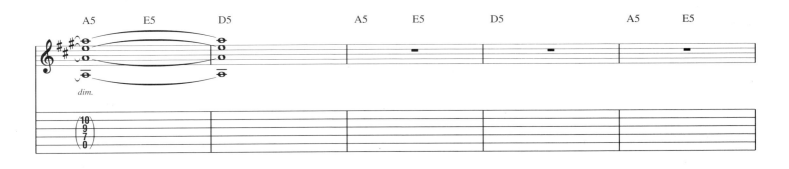

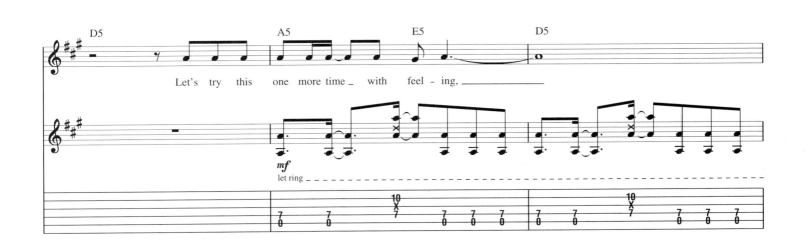

Let's try this one more time ___ with feel-ing, _____

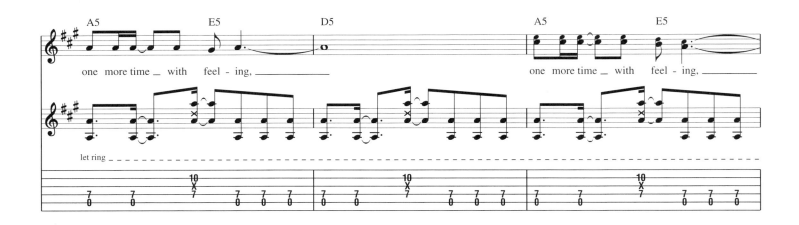

one more time _ with feel - ing, _____

one more time _ with feel - ing, _____

let ring _ _ _ _ _ _ _ _ _ _

D.S. al Coda

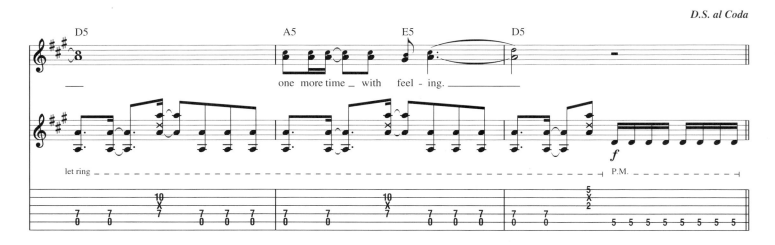

one more time _ with feel - ing. _____

let ring _ _ _ _ _ _ _ _ _ _ _ _ _ _   P.M. _ _ _ _ _ _ _ _ _

⊕ *Coda*

Outro
End Double-Time Feel

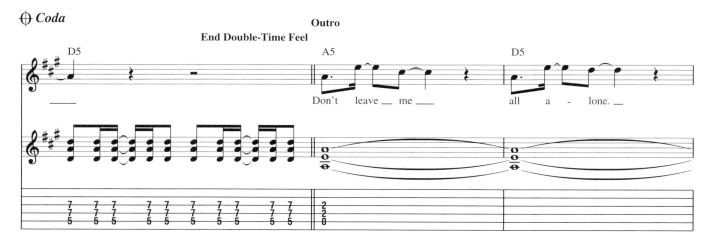

Don't leave _ me _ all a - lone. _

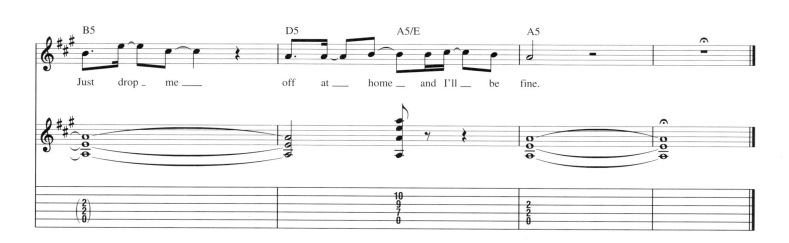

Just drop _ me _____ off at _ home _ and I'll _ be fine.

Aliens Exist

Words and Music by Tom DeLonge and Mark Hoppus

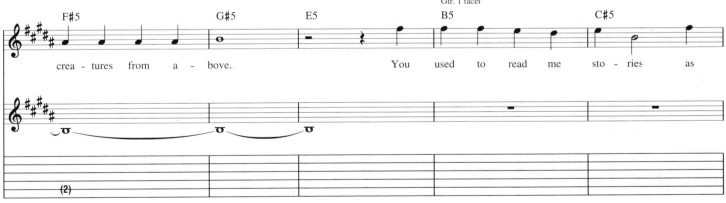

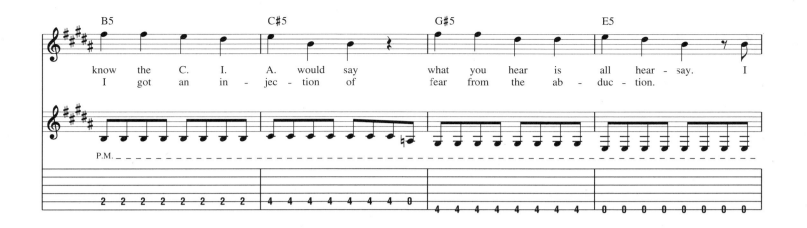

know the C. I. A. would say what you hear is all hear-say. I
I got an in-jec-tion of fear from the ab-duc-tion.

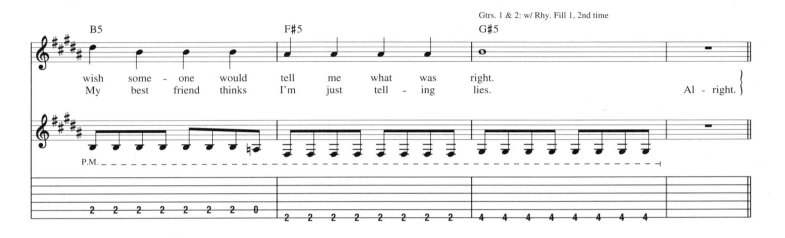

Gtrs. 1 & 2: w/ Rhy. Fill 1, 2nd time

wish some-one would tell me what was right.
My best friend thinks I'm just tell-ing lies. Al-right.

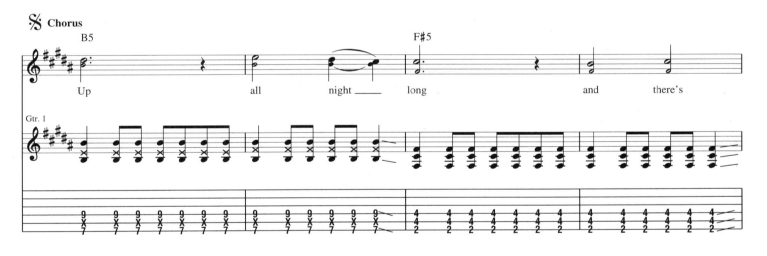

𝄋 Chorus

Up all night long and there's

Gtr. 1

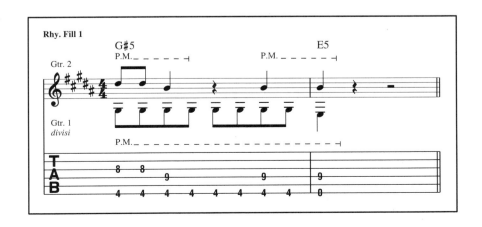

Rhy. Fill 1

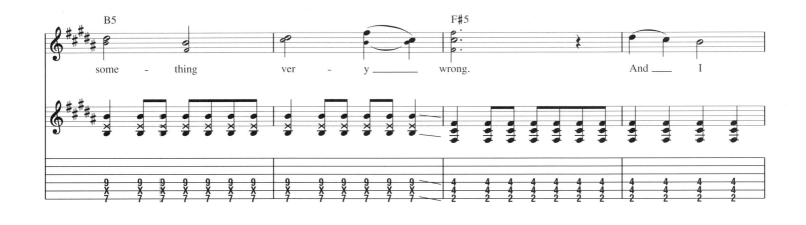

some - thing ver - y _____ wrong. And ___ I

know it must be late; been

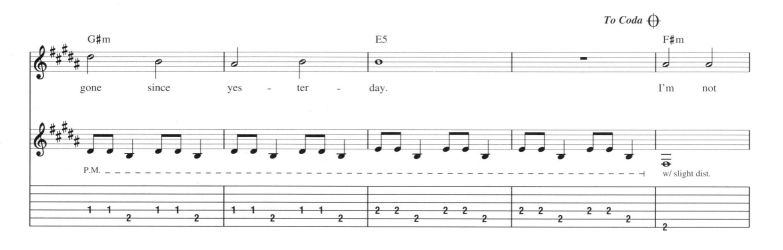

To Coda ⊕

gone since yes - ter - day. I'm not

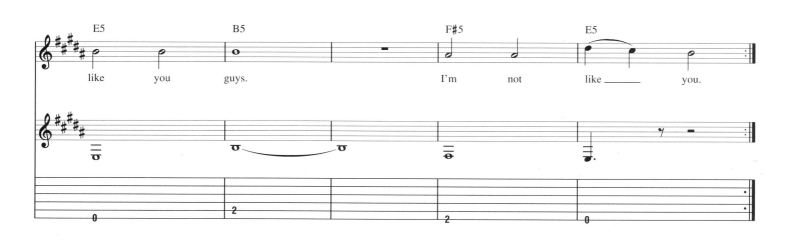

like you guys. I'm not like _____ you.

Going Away to College

Words and Music by Tom DeLonge and Mark Hoppus

she put up with my friends. I act - ed like an ass. I'd

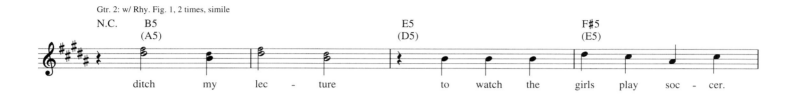

ditch my lec - ture to watch the girls play soc - cer.

D.S. al Coda 1

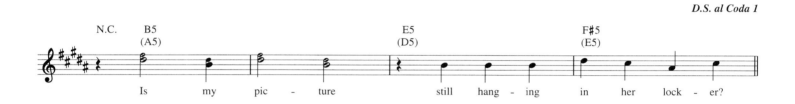

Is my pic - ture still hang - ing in her lock - er?

D.C. al Coda 2
(take repeat)

⊕ *Coda 1*

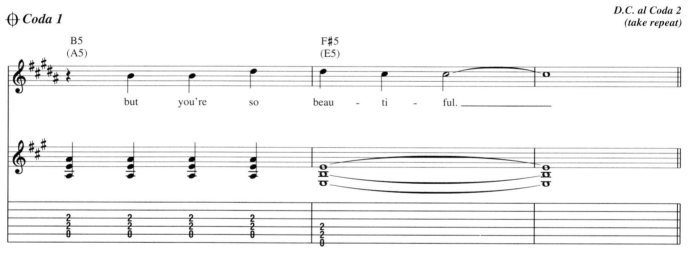

but you're so beau - ti - ful. _____

⊕ *Coda 2*

D.S. al Coda 3

⊕ *Coda 3*

Segue to "What's My Age Again?"

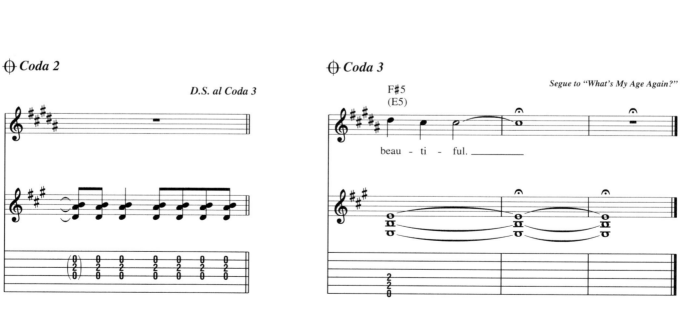

beau - ti - ful. _____

What's My Age Again?

Words and Music by Tom DeLonge and Mark Hoppus

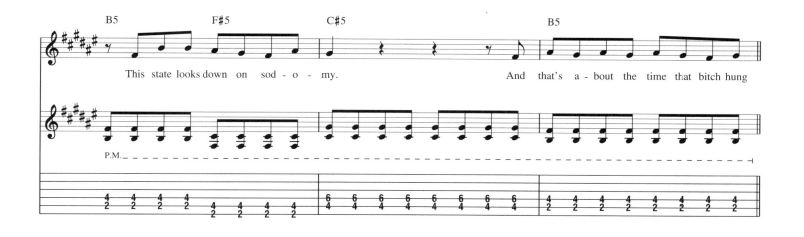

This state looks down on sod - o - my. And that's a - bout the time that bitch hung

Chorus

Gtr. 2: w/ Rhy. Fig. 1

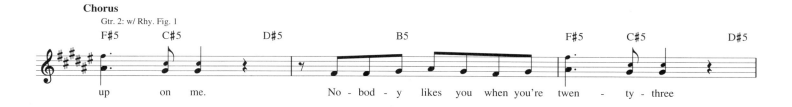

up on me. No - bod - y likes you when you're twen - ty - three

and are still more a - mused by prank phone calls. What the hell is call I - D? My

friends say I should act my age. What's my age a - gain? What's my age a - gain?

Interlude

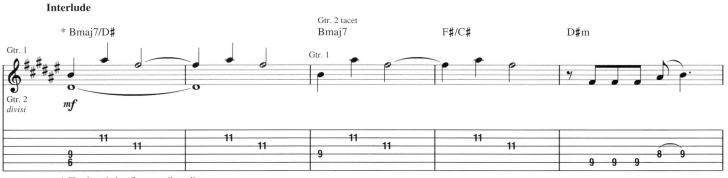

* Chord symbols reflect overall tonality.

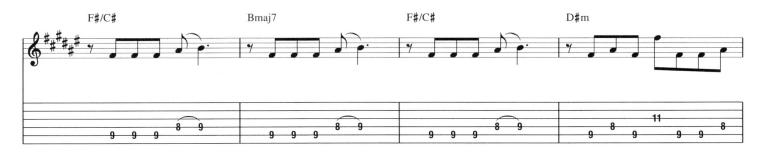

D.S. al Coda

And that's a - bout the time she walked a -

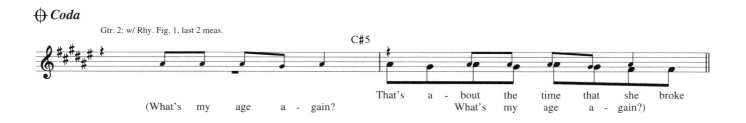

⊕ Coda

Gtr. 2: w/ Rhy. Fig. 1, last 2 meas.

C#5

(What's my age a - gain?

That's a - bout the time that she broke
What's my age a - gain?)

Chorus

Gtr. 2: w/ Rhy. Fig. 1

up   with me.   No one should take them-selves so   ser   -   i-ous-ly.
(Please   stay   with   me.   Please   stay

Gtr. 1

Riff B

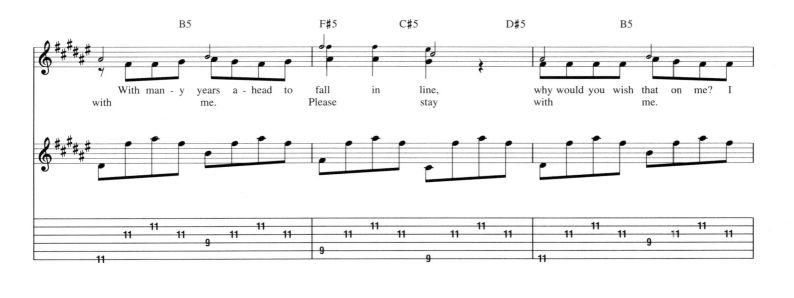

With man-y years a-head to fall in line, why would you wish that on me? I
with me. Please stay with me.

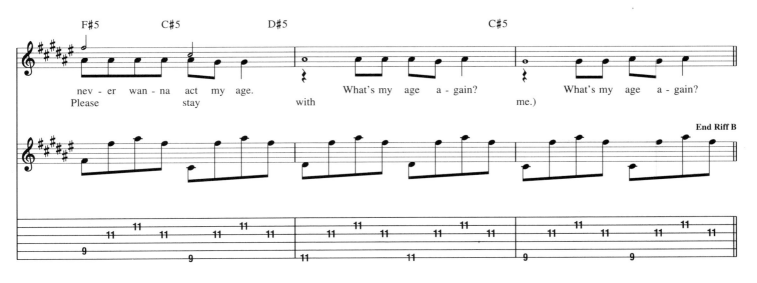

nev-er wan-na act my age. What's my age a-gain?
Please stay with me.) What's my age a-gain?

End Riff B

Outro
Gtr. 1: w/ Riff B
Gtr. 2: w/ Rhy. Fig. 1

play 3 times

What's my age a - gain? _____

Dysentery Gary

Words and Music by Tom DeLonge and Mark Hoppus

*Chord symbols reflect overall tonality.

Gtr. 4: w/ Riff B, 2 times

giv - ing ___ up. ___ She found some - one. There's

To Coda 2 ⊕

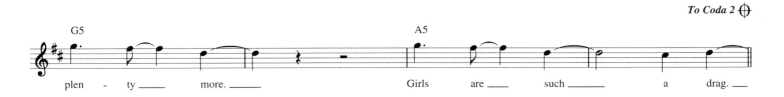

plen - ty ___ more. ___ Girls are ___ such ___ a drag. ___

Interlude

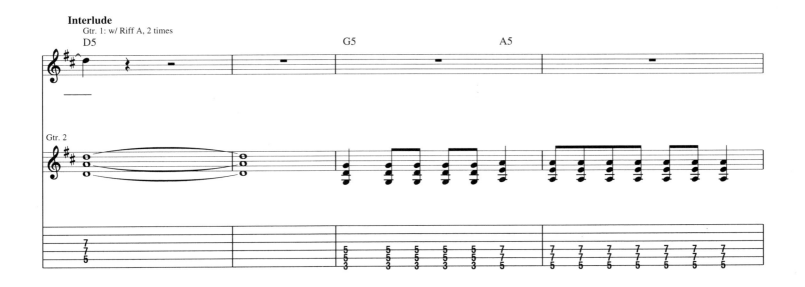

Gtr. 1: w/ Riff A, 2 times

Gtr. 2

D.S. al Coda 1

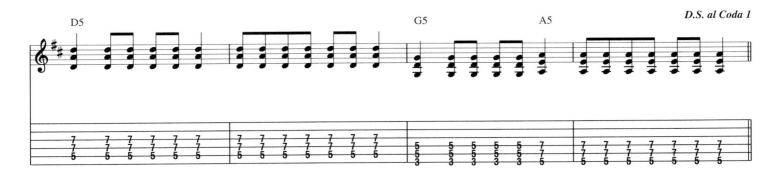

⊕ *Coda 1*

Bridge

Gtr. 2: w/ Rhy. Fig. 2

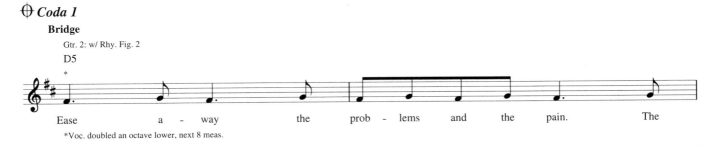

Ease a - way the prob – lems and the pain. The

*Voc. doubled an octave lower, next 8 meas.

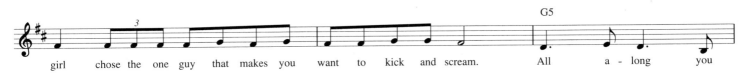

girl chose the one guy that makes you want to kick and scream. All a - long you

wish that she would stay. Fuck the guy that took and ran a - way. And...

⊕ *Coda 2*

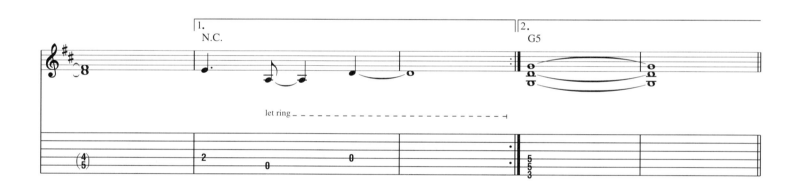

Chorus

Gtr. 3 tacet
Gtr. 4: w/ Riff B, 3 times

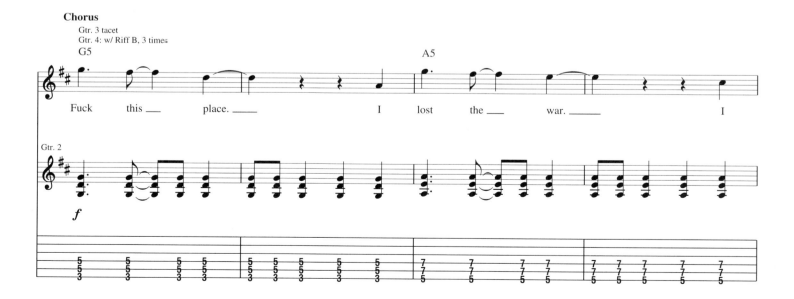

Fuck this __ place. __ I lost the __ war. _____ I

Adam's Song

Words and Music by Tom DeLonge and Mark Hoppus

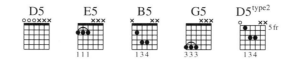

to go on. You'll be sor - ry when I'm ___
in the hall? ___ Please tell Mom this is not her ___

Interlude

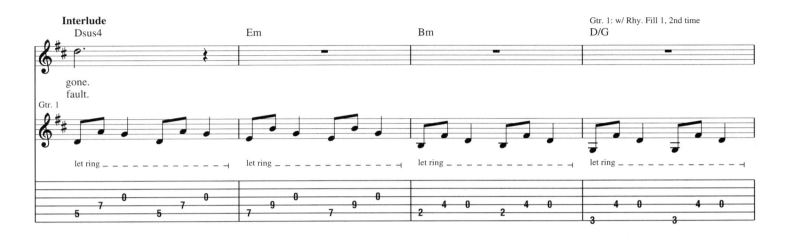

Gtr. 1: w/ Rhy. Fill 1, 2nd time

gone.
fault.

let ring

Gtr. 1: w/ Rhy. Fill 1, 2nd time

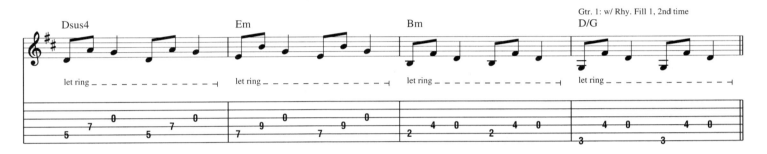

℅ Chorus

Gtrs. 1, 2 & 3: w/ Riffs A, A1 & A2, 2 times, 3rd time
Gtr. 4: w/ Rhy. Fig. 3, 2 times, 3rd time

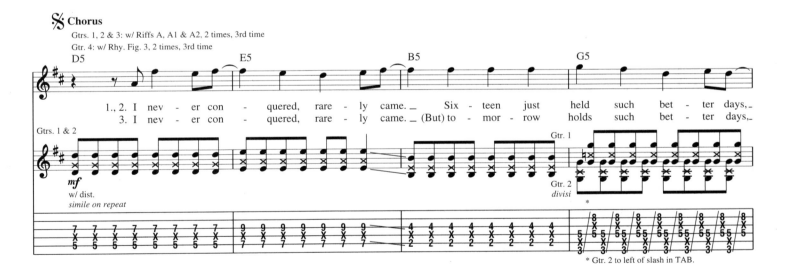

1., 2. I nev - er con - quered, rare - ly came. ___ Six - teen just held such bet - ter days, ___
3. I nev - er con - quered, rare - ly came. (But) to - mor - row holds such bet - ter days, ___

Gtrs. 1 & 2

mf
w/ dist.
simile on repeat

Gtr. 1

Gtr. 2
divisi
*

* Gtr. 2 to left of slash in TAB.

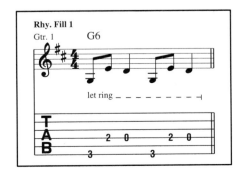

Rhy. Fill 1
Gtr. 1   G6

let ring

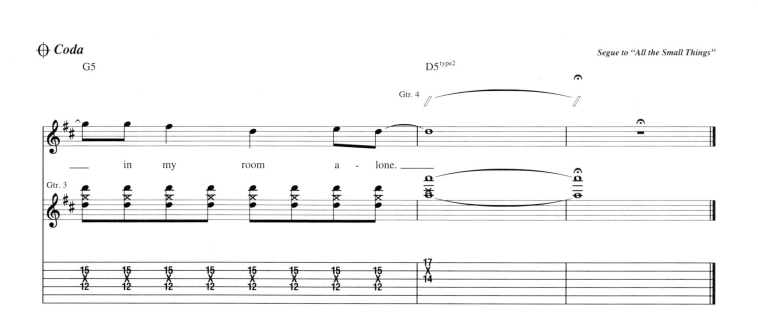

All the Small Things

Words and Music by Tom DeLonge and Mark Hoppus

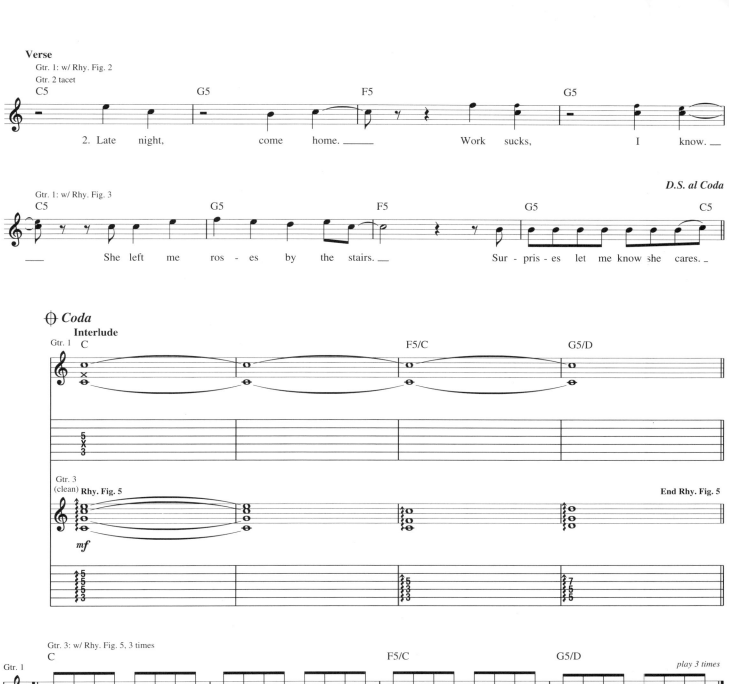

Verse

Gtr. 1: w/ Rhy. Fig. 2
Gtr. 2 tacet

2. Late night, come home. Work sucks, I know.

D.S. al Coda

Gtr. 1: w/ Rhy. Fig. 3

She left me ros - es by the stairs. Sur - pris - es let me know she cares.

⊕ Coda

Interlude

Gtr. 1

Gtr. 3 (clean) **Rhy. Fig. 5**

End Rhy. Fig. 5

mf

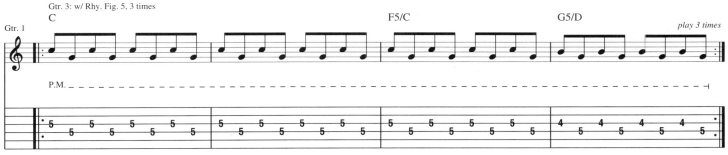

Gtr. 3: w/ Rhy. Fig. 5, 3 times

Gtr. 1

play 3 times

P.M.

Outro

Gtr. 1: w/ Rhy. Fig. 4, 2 times
Gtr. 2: w/ Riff A, 3 1/2 times

Say it ain't so. I will not __ go. Turn the lights __ off. Car - ry me __

home. Keep your head still. I'll be your __ thrill. The night will go __ on, my lit - tle wind -

The Party Song

Words and Music by Tom DeLonge and Mark Hoppus

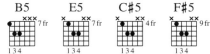

Intro

Fast Rock ♩ = 236
Double-Time Feel

1. "Do you want to come to a par-ty?" My friends picked me up in their truck at e-lev-en-thir-ty. "This

*doubled throughout

**Chord symbols reflect implied tonality.

Verse

thing's at a frat house, but peo-ple are cool there." Re-luc-tant, I fol-lowed, but

I nev-er dreamed there would be some-one there who would catch my at-ten-tion. I was-n't out search-ing for

love or af-fec-tion. So I paid my three and the girls got in free. Shined the beer for te-qui-la and

we head-ed in-to the par-ty. 2. And

Verse

Double-Time Feel

Gtr. 2: w/ Fill 1, 2nd time

B5   E5   C#5   E5

then in the back-yard, some ter - ri - ble ska band, some-one in the back-ground was do-ing a keg stand. This
could-n't be-lieve what this la - dy was say-ing, the names she was drop-ping, the games she was play-ing. She

Rhy. Fig. 1   End Rhy. Fig. 1

f

Gtr. 1: w/ Rhy. Fig. 1, 2 1/2 times

B5   E5   C#5

place is so lame, all these girls look the same, all these guys have no game. I wish
dat - ed this guy who now rides for Black Flys, how she's down with the wise well con -

E5   B5   E5

I would have stayed in my bed back at home, watch - ing T V a - lone, where I'd
struct - ed dis - guise. Now I'd rath - er go date - less than stay here and hate this. Her

C#5   E5   B5   E5

put on some porn or have sex on the phone, far from peo - ple I hate, down from an - y - where state, try'n' to
vol - ume of make-up, her fake tits were taste-less. So I said I'd call her but nev - er would both - er un -

End Double-Time Feel

C#5   E5   F#5   B5   N.C.

in - tox - i - cate girls to give them head af - ter the par - ty.
till I got turned down by an - oth - er girl at a par - ty.

Gtr. 1

Fill 1
Gtr. 2

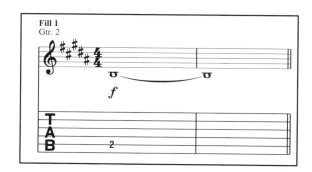

f

44

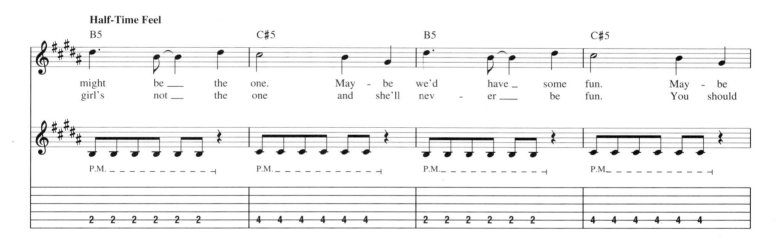

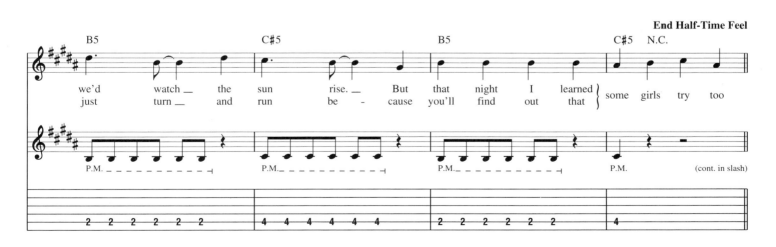

Mutt

Words and Music by Tom DeLonge, Mark Hoppus and Travis Barker

Verse

1. He paus - es shav - ing and he tells him - self that he is the bomb.
2. She smokes a doz - en and he does - n't seem to no - tice the smell.

**Chord symbols reflect implied tonality.

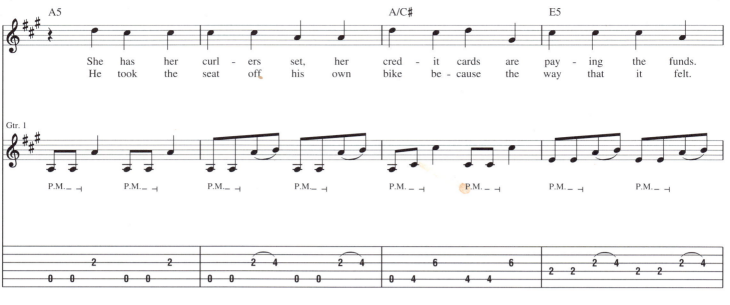

yeah. (And) they don't e - ven care at

Interlude

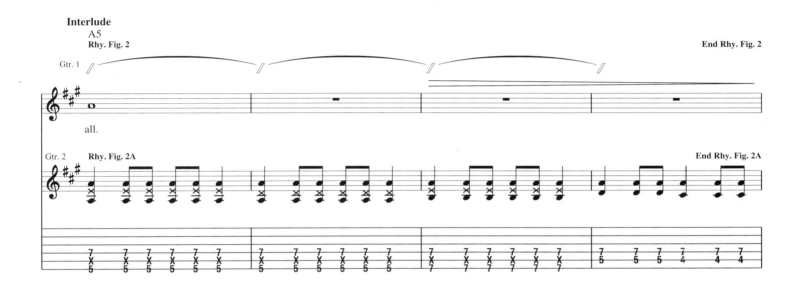

all.

Gtr. 1 tacet
Gtr. 2: w/ Rhy. Fig. 2A

𝄋𝄋 Chorus

Gtr. 1: w/ Rhy. Fig. 2, 3rd time
Gtr. 2: w/ Rhy. Fig. 2A, 4 times

Bkgd. Voc.: w/ Voc. Fig. 1, 2nd time, simile

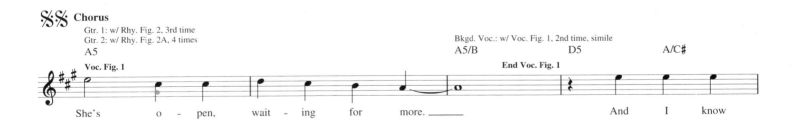

She's o - pen, wait - ing for more. And I know

Bkgd. Voc.: w/ Voc. Fig. 2, 2nd time

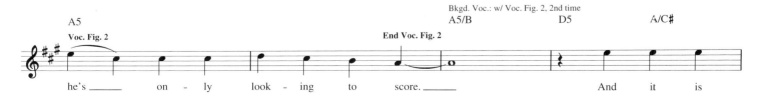

he's on - ly look - ing to score. And it is

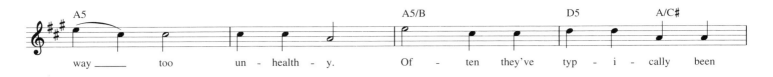

way ____ too un - health - y. Of - ten they've typ - i - cally been

starved for at - ten - tion be - fore. ____

To Coda 1 ⊕
To Coda 2 ⊕
D.S. al Coda 1
(take repeat)

⊕ *Coda 1*

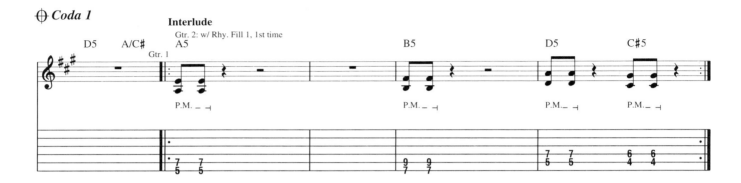

⊕ *Coda 2*

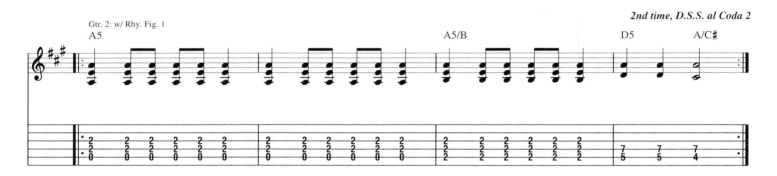

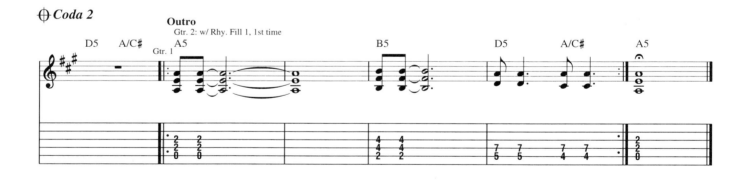

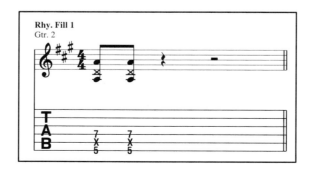

Wendy Clear

Words and Music by Tom DeLonge and Mark Hoppus

**composite arrangement.

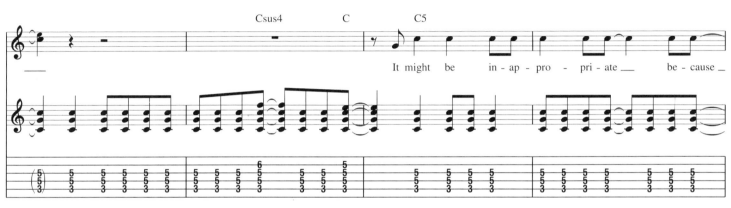

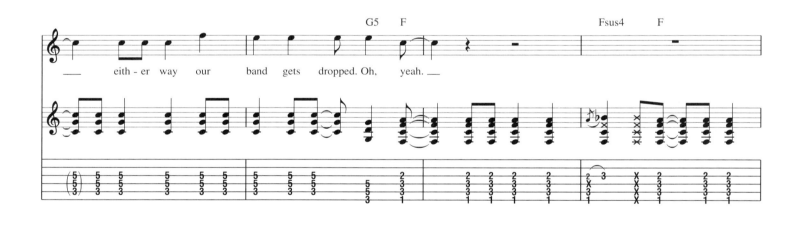

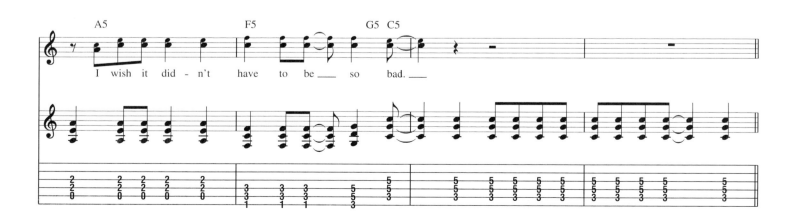

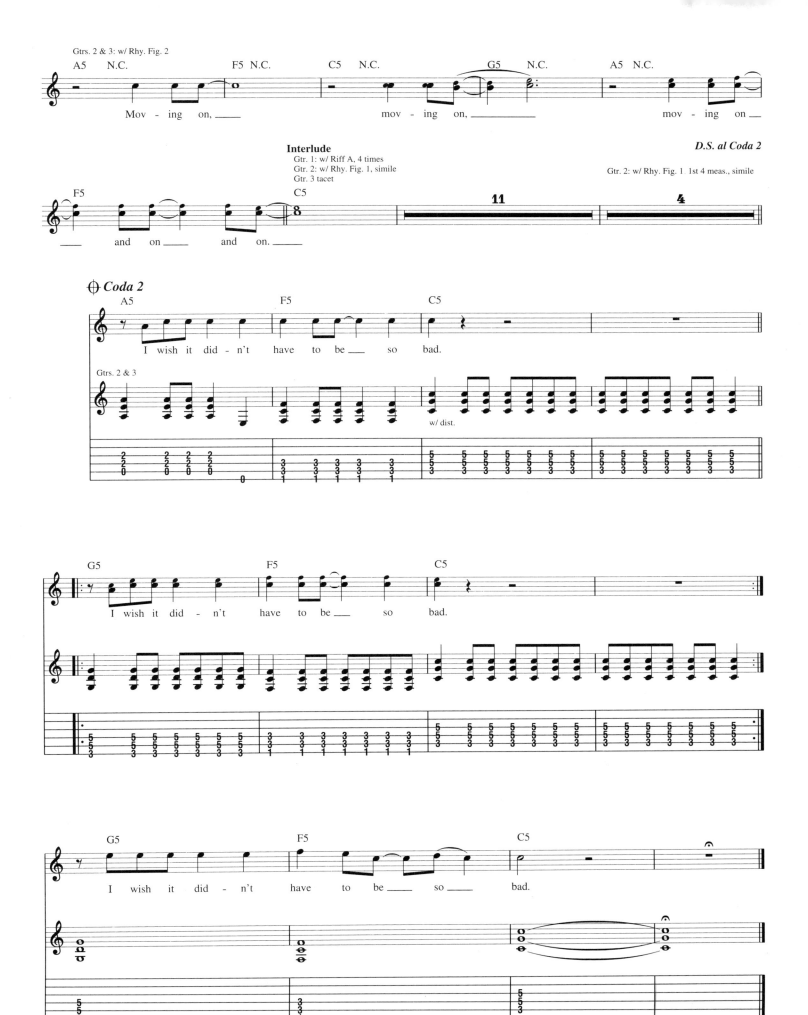

Anthem

Words and Music by Tom DeLonge and Mark Hoppus

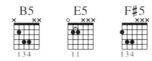

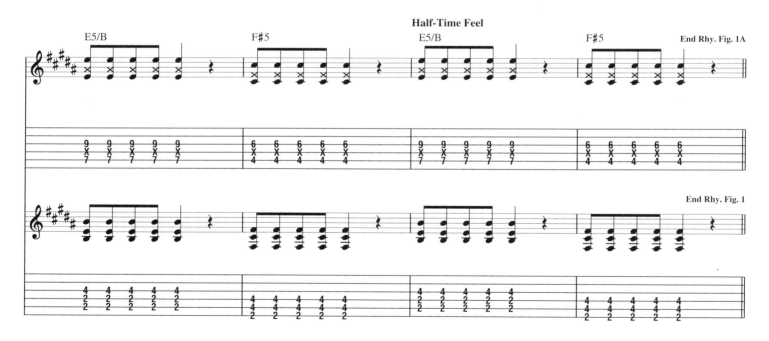

passed out on the floor. Third time, been caught

End Half-Time Feel

twice. For - give our neigh - bor, Bob. I think he humped the dog.

Chorus

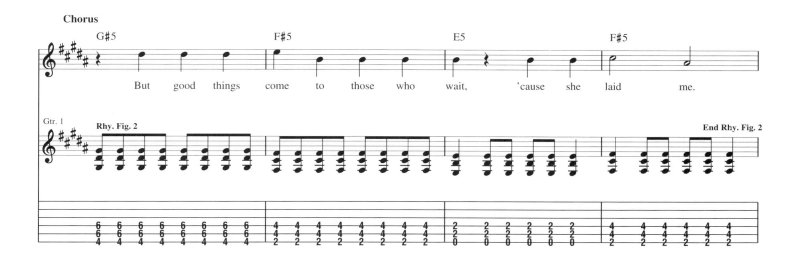

But good things come to those who wait, 'cause she laid me.

Gtr. 1: w/ Rhy. Fig. 2, 3 times, simile

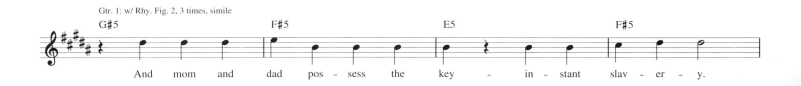

And mom and dad pos - sess the key — in - stant slav - er - y.

No need ex - plain the plan, no need to e - ven both - er.

I'll pack my bags, I swear I'll run. Wish my friends were twen - ty -

Gtrs. 1 & 2: w/ Rhy. Figs. 3 & 3A

How's _____ Chris marked with lip - stick?

Bet - ter call their fath - ers, sleep - ing with your daugh - ters.

§ **Chorus**

But good things come to those who wait, 'cause she laid me.

Gtr. 1 · Rhy. Fig. 4 _____ End Rhy. Fig. 4

Gtr. 1: w/ Rhy. Fig. 4, 2 3/4 times

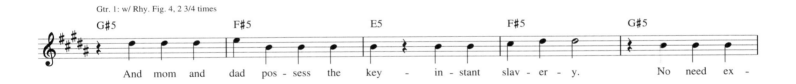

And mom and dad pos - sess the key - in - stant slav - er - y. No need ex -

plain the plan, no need to e - ven both - er. I'll pack my bags, I swear I'll run. Wish my

End Double-Time Feel **Bridge**
Half-Time Feel

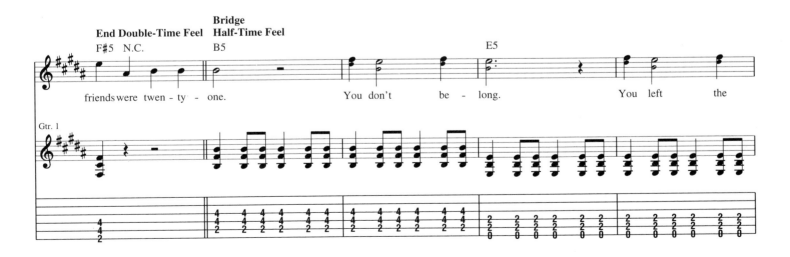

friends were twen - ty - one. You don't be - long. You left the

Gtr. 1

Interlude

**End Double-Time Feel

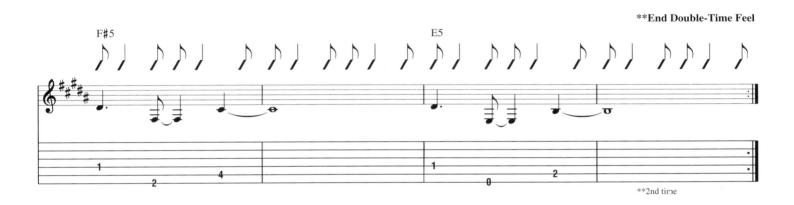

**2nd time

Interlude

*Bass arr. for gtr.

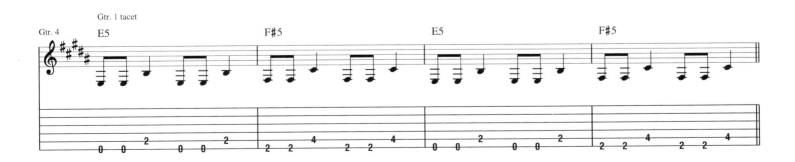

Guitar Notation Legend

Guitar Music can be notated three different ways: on a *musical staff*, in *tablature*, and in *rhythm slashes*.

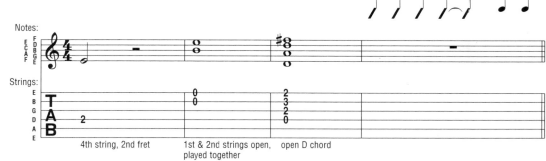

RHYTHM SLASHES are written above the staff. Strum chords in the rhythm indicated. Use the chord diagrams found at the top of the first page of the transcription for the appropriate chord voicings. Round noteheads indicate single notes.

THE MUSICAL STAFF shows pitches and rhythms and is divided by bar lines into measures. Pitches are named after the first seven letters of the alphabet.

TABLATURE graphically represents the guitar fingerboard. Each horizontal line represents a string, and each number represents a fret.

HALF-STEP BEND: Strike the note and bend up 1/2 step.

WHOLE-STEP BEND: Strike the note and bend up one step.

GRACE NOTE BEND: Strike the note and bend up as indicated. The first note does not take up any time.

SLIGHT (MICROTONE) BEND: Strike the note and bend up 1/4 step.

BEND AND RELEASE: Strike the note and bend up as indicated, then release back to the original note. Only the first note is struck.

PRE-BEND: Bend the note as indicated, then strike it.

VIBRATO: The string is vibrated by rapidly bending and releasing the note with the fretting hand.

WIDE VIBRATO: The pitch is varied to a greater degree by vibrating with the fretting hand.

HAMMER-ON: Strike the first (lower) note with one finger, then sound the higher note (on the same string) with another finger by fretting it without picking.

PULL-OFF: Place both fingers on the notes to be sounded. Strike the first note and without picking, pull the finger off to sound the second (lower) note.

LEGATO SLIDE: Strike the first note and then slide the same fret-hand finger up or down to the second note. The second note is not struck.

SHIFT SLIDE: Same as legato slide, except the second note is struck.

TRILL: Very rapidly alternate between the notes indicated by continuously hammering on and pulling off.

TAPPING: Hammer ("tap") the fret indicated with the pick-hand index or middle finger and pull off to the note fretted by the fret hand.

NATURAL HARMONIC: Strike the note while the fret-hand lightly touches the string directly over the fret indicated.

PINCH HARMONIC: The note is fretted normally and a harmonic is produced by adding the edge of the thumb or the tip of the index finger of the pick hand to the normal pick attack.

PICK SCRAPE: The edge of the pick is rubbed down (or up) the string, producing a scratchy sound.

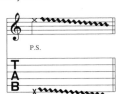

MUFFLED STRINGS: A percussive sound is produced by laying the fret hand across the string(s) without depressing, and striking them with the pick hand.

PALM MUTING: The note is partially muted by the pick hand lightly touching the string(s) just before the bridge.

RAKE: Drag the pick across the strings indicated with a single motion.

TREMOLO PICKING: The note is picked as rapidly and continuously as possible.

VIBRATO BAR DIVE AND RETURN: The pitch of the note or chord is dropped a specified number of steps (in rhythm) then returned to the original pitch.

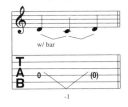

VIBRATO BAR SCOOP: Depress the bar just before striking the note, then quickly release the bar.

VIBRATO BAR DIP: Strike the note and then immediately drop a specified number of steps, then release back to the original pitch.

RECORDED VERSIONS
The Best Note-For-Note Transcriptions Available

RECORDED VERSIONS GUITAR

ALL BOOKS INCLUDE TABLATURE

00690016	Will Ackerman Collection	$19.95
00690199	Aerosmith – Nine Lives	$19.95
00690146	Aerosmith – Toys in the Attic	$19.95
00694865	Alice In Chains – Dirt	$19.95
00694932	Allman Brothers Band – Volume 1	$24.95
00694933	Allman Brothers Band – Volume 2	$24.95
00694934	Allman Brothers Band – Volume 3	$24.95
00694877	Chet Atkins – Guitars For All Seasons	$19.95
00694918	Randy Bachman Collection	$22.95
00694880	Beatles – Abbey Road	$19.95
00694863	Beatles – Sgt. Pepper's Lonely Hearts Club Band	$19.95
00690383	Beatles – Yellow Submarine	$19.95
00690174	Beck – Mellow Gold	$17.95
00690346	Beck – Mutations	$19.95
00690175	Beck – Odelay	$17.95
00694884	The Best of George Benson	$19.95
00692385	Chuck Berry	$19.95
00692200	Black Sabbath – We Sold Our Soul For Rock 'N' Roll	$19.95
00690115	Blind Melon – Soup	$19.95
00690305	Blink 182 – Dude Ranch	$19.95
00690028	Blue Oyster Cult – Cult Classics	$19.95
00690219	Blur	$19.95
00694935	Boston: Double Shot Of	$22.95
00690237	Meredith Brooks – Blurring the Edges	$19.95
00690168	Roy Buchanon Collection	$19.95
00690364	Cake – Songbook	$19.95
00690337	Jerry Cantrell – Boggy Depot	$19.95
00690293	Best of Steven Curtis Chapman	$19.95
00690043	Cheap Trick – Best Of	$19.95
00690171	Chicago – Definitive Guitar Collection	$22.95
00690393	Eric Clapton – Selections from Blues	$19.95
00660139	Eric Clapton – Journeyman	$19.95
00694869	Eric Clapton – Live Acoustic	$19.95
00694896	John Mayall/Eric Clapton – Bluesbreakers	$19.95
00690162	Best of the Clash	$19.95
00690166	Albert Collins – The Alligator Years	$16.95
00694940	Counting Crows – August & Everything After	$19.95
00690197	Counting Crows – Recovering the Satellites	$19.95
00690118	Cranberries – The Best of	$19.95
00690215	Music of Robert Cray	$19.95
00694840	Cream – Disraeli Gears	$19.95
00690352	Creed – My Own Pirson	$19.95
00690007	Danzig 4	$19.95
00690184	dc Talk – Jesus Freak	$19.95
00690333	dc Talk – Supernatural	$19.95
00660186	Alex De Grassi Guitar Collection	$19.95
00690289	Best of Deep Purple	$17.95
00694831	Derek And The Dominos – Layla & Other Assorted Love Songs	$19.95
00690322	Ani Di Franco – Little Plastic Castle	$19.95
00690187	Dire Straits – Brothers In Arms	$19.95
00690191	Dire Straits – Money For Nothing	$24.95
00695382	The Very Best of Dire Straits – Sultans of Swing	$19.95
00660178	Willie Dixon – Master Blues Composer	$24.95
00690250	Best of Duane Eddy	$16.95
00690349	Eve 6	$19.95
00690323	Fastball – All the Pain Money Can Buy	$19.95
00690089	Foo Fighters	$19.95
00690235	Foo Fighters – The Colour and the Shape	$19.95
00690394	Foo Fighters – There Is Nothing Left to Lose	$19.95
00694920	Free – Best Of	$18.95
00690324	Fuel – Sunburn	$19.95
00690222	G3 Live – Satriani, Vai, Johnson	$22.95

00694807	Danny Gatton – 88 Elmira St	$19.95
00690127	Goo Goo Dolls – A Boy Named Goo	$19.95
00690338	Goo Goo Dolls – Dizzy Up the Girl	$19.95
00690117	John Gorka Collection	$19.95
00690114	Buddy Guy Collection Vol. A-J	$22.95
00690193	Buddy Guy Collection Vol. L-Y	$22.95
00694798	George Harrison Anthology	$19.95
00690068	Return Of The Hellecasters	$19.95
00692930	Jimi Hendrix – Are You Experienced?	$24.95
00692931	Jimi Hendrix – Axis: Bold As Love	$22.95
00692932	Jimi Hendrix – Electric Ladyland	$24.95
00690218	Jimi Hendrix – First Rays of the New Rising Sun	$24.95
00690038	Gary Hoey – Best Of	$19.95
00660029	Buddy Holly	$19.95
00660169	John Lee Hooker – A Blues Legend	$19.95
00690054	Hootie & The Blowfish – Cracked Rear View	$19.95
00694905	Howlin' Wolf	$19.95
00690136	Indigo Girls – 1200 Curfews	$22.95
00694938	Elmore James – Master Electric Slide Guitar	$19.95
00690167	Skip James Blues Guitar Collection	$16.95
00694833	Billy Joel For Guitar	$19.95
00694912	Eric Johnson – Ah Via Musicom	$19.95
00690169	Eric Johnson – Venus Isle	$22.95
00694799	Robert Johnson – At The Crossroads	$19.95
00693185	Judas Priest – Vintage Hits	$19.95
00690277	Best of Kansas	$19.95
00690073	B. B. King – 1950-1957	$24.95
00690098	B. B. King – 1958-1967	$24.95
00690134	Freddie King Collection	$17.95
00694903	Best Of Kiss	$24.95
00690157	Kiss – Alive	$19.95
00690163	Mark Knopfler/Chet Atkins – Neck and Neck	$19.95
00690296	Patty Larkin Songbook	$17.95
00690070	Live – Throwing Copper	$19.95
00690018	Living Colour – Best Of	$19.95
00694845	Yngwie Malmsteen – Fire And Ice	$19.95
00694956	Bob Marley – Legend	$19.95
00690283	Best of Sarah McLachlan	$19.95
00690382	Sarah McLachlan – Mirrorball	$19.95
00690354	Sarah McLachlan – Surfacing	$19.95
00690239	Matchbox 20 – Yourself or Someone Like You	$19.95
00690244	Megadeath – Cryptic Writings	$19.95
00690236	Mighty Mighty Bosstones – Let's Face It	$19.95
00690040	Steve Miller Band Greatest Hits	$19.95
00694802	Gary Moore – Still Got The Blues	$19.95
00694958	Mountain, Best Of	$19.95
00694913	Nirvana – In Utero	$19.95
00694883	Nirvana – Nevermind	$19.95
00690026	Nirvana – Acoustic In New York	$19.95
00690121	Oasis – (What's The Story) Morning Glory	$19.95
00690290	Offspring, The – Ignition	$19.95
00690204	Offspring, The – Ixnay on the Hombre	$17.95
00690203	Offspring, The – Smash	$17.95
00694830	Ozzy Osbourne – No More Tears	$19.95
00694855	Pearl Jam – Ten	$19.95
00690053	Liz Phair – Whip Smart	$19.95
00690176	Phish – Billy Breathes	$22.95
00690331	Phish – The Story of Ghost	$19.95
00693800	Pink Floyd – Early Classics	$19.95
00694967	Police – Message In A Box Boxed Set	$70.00
00694974	Queen – A Night At The Opera	$19.95
00690395	Rage Against The Machine – The Battle of Los Angeles	$19.95
00690145	Rage Against The Machine – Evil Empire	$19.95
00690179	Rancid – And Out Come the Wolves	$22.95

00690055	Red Hot Chili Peppers – Bloodsugarsexmagik	$19.95
00690379	Red Hot Chili Peppers – Californication	$19.95
00690090	Red Hot Chili Peppers – One Hot Minute	$22.95
00694892	Guitar Style Of Jerry Reed	$19.95
00694937	Jimmy Reed – Master Bluesman	$19.95
00694899	R.E.M. – Automatic For The People	$19.95
00690260	Jimmie Rodgers Guitar Collection	$17.95
00690014	Rolling Stones – Exile On Main Street	$24.95
00690186	Rolling Stones – Rock & Roll Circus	$19.95
00690135	Otis Rush Collection	$19.95
00690031	Santana's Greatest Hits	$19.95
00694805	Scorpions – Crazy World	$19.95
00690150	Son Seals – Bad Axe Blues	$17.95
00690128	Seven Mary Three – American Standards	$19.95
00690076	Sex Pistols – Never Mind The Bollocks	$19.95
00120105	Kenny Wayne Shepherd – Ledbetter Heights	$19.95
00120123	Kenny Wayne Shepherd – Trouble Is	$19.95
00690196	Silverchair – Freak Show	$19.95
00690130	Silverchair – Frogstomp	$19.95
00690041	Smithereens – Best Of	$19.95
00694885	Spin Doctors – Pocket Full Of Kryptonite	$19.95
00690124	Sponge – Rotting Pinata	$19.95
00694921	Steppenwolf, The Best Of	$22.95
00694957	Rod Stewart – Acoustic Live	$22.95
00690021	Sting – Fields Of Gold	$19.95
00690242	Suede – Coming Up	$19.95
00694824	Best Of James Taylor	$16.95
00690238	Third Eye Blind	$19.95
00690267	311	$19.95
00690030	Toad The Wet Sprocket	$19.95
00690228	Tonic – Lemon Parade	$19.95
00690295	Tool – Aenima	$19.95
00699191	The Best of U2 – 1980-1990	$19.95
00694411	U2 – The Joshua Tree	$19.95
00690039	Steve Vai – Alien Love Secrets	$24.95
00690172	Steve Vai – Fire Garden	$24.95
00690023	Jimmie Vaughan – Strange Pleasures	$19.95
00690370	Stevie Ray Vaughan and Double Trouble – The Real Deal: Greatest Hits Volume 2	$22.95
00660136	Stevie Ray Vaughan – In Step	$19.95
00694835	Stevie Ray Vaughan – The Sky Is Crying	$19.95
00694776	Vaughan Brothers – Family Style	$19.95
00690217	Verve Pipe, The – Villains	$19.95
00120026	Joe Walsh – Look What I Did	$24.95
00694789	Muddy Waters – Deep Blues	$24.95
00690071	Weezer	$19.95
00690286	Weezer – Pinkerton	$19.95
00694970	Who, The – Definitive Collection A-E	$24.95
00694971	Who, The – Definitive Collection F-Li	$24.95
00694972	Who, The – Definitive Collection Lo-R	$24.95
00694973	Who, The – Definitive Collection S-Y	$24.95
00690320	Best of Dar Williams	$17.95
00690319	Best of Stevie Wonder	$19.95
00690319	Stevie Wonder – Some of the Best	$19.95